THE
ADVISOR'S
MINEFIELD

*WHY PROFESSIONAL FIRMS
ARE SUED & HOW TO
PROTECT YOUR PRACTICE*

SHAUN TRACEY

ELITE PROFESSIONAL RISK

Published by ELITE PROFESSIONAL RISK, LLC

Publisher's website: www.eliteprofessionalrisk.com

Information on this title: www.advisorsminefield.com

Acknowledgements

Cover design: Soledad Ludueña of Luna Design
Internal design: Amna Jehangir
Copyediting: Emma Moylan
Narration of audiobook edition: Michael Hajiantonis, Rachel Capell & Amy Weaver

Disclaimer

1) This publication is designed to provide accurate and authoritative guidance in regard to the subject matter covered as at the date of publication. It is sold on the understanding that neither the publisher nor the author is engaged in rendering professional services via this book. If professional advice is required, the services of a competent professional should be sought. Likewise, it does not purport to address the professional rules, regulations and/or requirements of any particular profession in any particular jurisdiction.

2) Save where stated to the contrary, the stories in this book are fictional. Likewise, except in the Preface and Introduction, the author's use of the personal pronoun does not depict real-life events.

3) This publication has been written and created entirely without the use of alternative intelligence or 'AI'.

Ordering information

Special editions and volume discounts are available for bulk purchases by firms, associations and others. For details, please contact the publisher at: info@eliteprofessionalrisk.com.

THE ADVISOR'S MINEFIELD/Shaun Tracey First Edition.

ISBN Hardback: 979-8-9988951-0-4

ISBN Paperback: 979-8-9988951-1-1

ISBN E-book: 979-8-9988951-2-8

ISBN Audiobook: 979-8-9988951-3-5

For special editions, bulk orders, and speaking and training engagements, please contact info@eliteprofessionalrisk.com

To subscribe to the *Advisor's Minefield* podcast, please visit www.advisorsminefield.com or your usual podcast provider including Apple Podcasts and Spotify.

Contents

PREFACE

While there are many guides to becoming a trusted advisor and succeeding in your professional career, little has been written for practitioners about how to avoid the one major risk that pervades all of professional practice: the risk of being sued by a client.

Whenever a professional firm is sued, the claim may be worth millions or even billions and yet, for the 'accused' advisors, the claim is also deeply personal. These advisors, typically experts in their field, suddenly face allegations of negligence or even wilful breach of duty.

However supportive their firm may be, the claim brings heavy pressure and is even a threat to the advisors' mental health.

Having acted as defence counsel to many well-known firms in 'big-money' lawsuits, I have an insider's perspective on why even elite firms are sued, the staggering cost of the claims, and the lessons that may help practitioners to avoid such a professional crisis.

In each case, I become immersed in a lengthy litigation process that begins with interviewing the 'accused' advisors. During those first conversations, some advisors are visibly shaken by what appears to have been a rare lapse on their part,

1

whereas others are indignant at being blamed unjustly for their clients' problems.

Liability litigation also involves deep-dive file reviews, discovery of all relevant documents, and building the firm's best defence through witness evidence and legal arguments. Although some disputes settle out of court, other claims reach trial, in which case the advisors testify under oath and the court renders its verdict.

Whatever the merits of the claim, facing such a lawsuit causes immense personal and financial costs, and reputations are always on the line.

However, in my experience there is barely any feedback loop by which practitioners get to know the causes and costs of liability claims. Regrettably, the sensitivities involved, and the tendency for claims to settle confidentially, mean the wider professional community learns little about what went wrong, why and how the claims could have been avoided.

To promote a liability feedback loop, I share insights drawn directly from my twenty years of practice as defence counsel to show why advisors are sued and how they can strive to avoid, or at least robustly defend, such claims.

The Advisor's Minefield is not a legal textbook, as I take a story-based, practical approach, using adapted and anonymized scenarios where necessary to preserve confidentiality. The core stories in Chapters 1–3 feature claims against law firms and accountants; however, the lessons in this book generally apply across the advisory professions, including in financial services, insurance brokerage, tax advisory, property valuation, and construction projects.

Further, practice-specific guidance is also now available through my Elite Professional Risk training courses. These courses help firms to ensure that advisory staff at all levels know about the causes and costs of these claims and how best to protect their firm.

I welcome your engagement with these concerns and invite you to subscribe to the *Advisor's Minefield* podcast for related content including expert interviews and emerging trends.

Shaun Tracey

E: shaun@eliteprofessionalrisk.com

15 September 2025

THE ADVISOR'S MINEFIELD

'It was deadline day, wasn't it, Mr Moore?'

'It was.'

'And you had a lot on your plate?'

'I did.'

'You were under pressure to approve all the reports due that day, weren't you, Mr Moore?'

'I was.'

'And you approved *this* report without caring about its contents, didn't you, Mr Moore?'

'No, of course I cared.'

'The truth is you would have signed off on *anything*, wouldn't you, Mr Moore, just to get this report off your desk?'

'Absolutely not.'

'No further questions, My Lord.'

* * *

As professional advisors, we handle complex issues, constant emails, pressing deadlines, demanding clients and one overriding expectation: we will always get things right.

Indeed, there are few more serious concerns for any advisor than no longer being trusted as a safe pair of hands, let alone facing a liability lawsuit.

It is no exaggeration to say that being cross-examined at trial is every professional's worst nightmare.

As a specialist in defending leading firms that are sued by their clients, I see careers derailed by these claims and massive sums paid in settlement.

Deep-pocket defendants

Even the leading professional firms are sued far more frequently than one might imagine. Their risk policies are all in place, but the claims keep coming. I once acted for a law firm sued by three different clients within six months, in each case for several million pounds. All three claims were settled but the costs did not simply fall to the firm's insurers as the firm's insurance deductible was £500,000 per claim.

Mega-deals can lead to mega-claims and the fallout is always costly:

- for firms, every lawsuit threatens their reputation, client relationships and bottom line;

- for insurers, the flow of claims can become an expensive flood; and

- for the advisors themselves, a claim means stress, stigma and a career setback.

The examples given in this book include a billion-dollar claim caused by a contract containing a single mistaken word.

Claims in the billions are rare but, when they do hit, they blow a firm's insurance cover and threaten its very existence.

The most striking collapse of a professional firm remains the sudden demise of the 'big five' accountancy firm Arthur Andersen, former auditor of the US energy company Enron, following the emergence in 2001 of the Enron fraud, which cost its investors over US$60 billion.

More recently, HSBC entities were sued for US$2 billion by the liquidators of Primeo Fund, an offshore investment fund that placed all of its money with the fraudster Bernard L. Madoff. HSBC, for whom I act as a member of its legal defence team, had served as fund custodian and administrator for Primeo, and the claims concerned alleged failures by HSBC in the performance of its professional duties.

Although HSBC successfully defended the claims at every judicial level, including the Judicial Committee of the Privy Council, the litigation lasted for a decade and the costs and complexity were immense. More than eighty thousand documents were disclosed by the parties, the first-instance trial ran for twelve weeks, and the court heard contested evidence from twenty-eight witnesses including a former director of the FBI.

At the time of writing, a US$2.7 billion claim made against Ernst & Young LLP is being heard at a five-month High Court trial in London. The claimants are the administrators of a failed UAE healthcare provider, NMC Health Plc, a former FTSE 100 listed company that reportedly collapsed in 2020 after disclosing more than US$4 billion in hidden debt. The core claim is that EY acted in breach of duty by issuing unqualified audit reports on NMC's accounts from 2012 until 2018 and failing to gain access to key books and records of NMC that would have revealed the fraud. EY has denied liability on the grounds that the fraud was perpetrated by senior personnel at NMC who manipulated its accounts and prevented EY from obtaining all books and records. The outcome of this complex case is awaited with interest.

Claims the millions are frequent and cause large losses for the defendant firms. Not only must each firm pay its insurance policy deductible, but it also spends valuable time defending the claim, suffers a damaged client relationship, and fears negative press.

Such lawsuits are brought with regularity against law firms, accountants, tax advisors, brokers, surveyors, architects and other advisors.

Then there is the depressing flow of smaller claims, notified to insurers rather like traffic accidents, except reputations are always at stake.

Some liability claims are genuine and well founded, where an error has regrettably been made.

However, professional firms are also vulnerable to scapegoat claims where they are sued despite having given the right advice; if the advisor has not fully protected their position, the firm may struggle to defend the claim.

The need to protect yourself and your firm

Early in my career, whenever I read a headline about advisors being sued, I sympathized but also held an unspoken assumption that liability claims were for *other people*; for small firms, the unlucky, or an incompetent few.

However, this was wishful thinking. Now, having defended senior partners, experts and rainmakers from the best firms, I know pedigree, competence and diligence offer no immunity.

Any advisor may make a rare mistake or be sued by their client even if they were careful, and even if they gave the right advice.

The key to avoiding claims lies not only within formal risk management policies, but also in advisors handling professional risk astutely under pressure.

Claims prevention also involves appreciating:

- why a client might sue your firm, even though they value your advice;

- which three major problems any client could face, and why each of them could lead to a claim against your firm; and

- how a client could blame you for their own mistake, misjudgement or misfortune.

Lessons through stories

No one relishes a risk manual, but everyone loves a story.

Through stories based upon lawsuits brought against leading professional firms, I explain how and why top-class advisors are sued by their clients, and the valuable lessons for practitioners.

Chapters 1–3 contain core stories that show not only the causes of the claims, but also the aftermath for the advisors and factors that help or hinder their firm's defence.

Chapter 4 then explains the three main reasons that clients sue their advisors, and Chapter 5 briefly covers the four main client reactions to major problems.

Chapters 6 and 7 address the dynamics of scapegoat claims, including how advisors can best protect themselves against the risk of being unfairly blamed for their clients' problems.

Chapters 8 and 9 suggest how certain warning signs, or 'red flags', may indicate an elevated risk of making an error that could result in a liability claim.

The conclusion draws together the broad lessons from the claims featured in this book and provides a short recap by way of summary.

Finally, the appendices suggest next steps for practitioners and at a firm management level.

* * *

Despite its sobering stories, *The Advisor's Minefield* has a positive message: many lawsuits can be avoided, or at least robustly defended, by protecting yourself and your firm during your professional career.

CHAPTER 1

'PURELY HIGH LEVEL'

'S tulba advokati. Idioti!'

Berzin threw his phone overboard and slammed his fist against the wheel of his yacht.

Berzin's phone plopped into the water as his boat bobbed on the calm Mediterranean Sea.

'Darling, what's wrong?' asked Berzin's wife.

'Damn lawyers! Idiots! The yacht deal. They've lost me twelve million that was guaranteed. Twelve million!'

'How?'

'Stupidity! Bring me your phone.'

* * *

'Mr Berzin, thank you for contacting me, and I'm very sorry to hear about this problem,' said Steven Polk, a seasoned litigation attorney. 'Yes, I would be glad to represent you in this matter. It sounds like you have lost out through no fault of your own. Firms like Davis & Hendry have many millions worth of insurance coverage for mistakes just like this. Please tell me more about what has happened.'

'Yes, of course, I will explain as clearly as I can. I buy and sell assets—companies, ships, aircraft, and so on. I buy cheap and sell expensive. I flip the assets quickly for a big profit.'

'And this time you were buying a yacht?' Polk asked.

'Yes, a superyacht. I buy for $18 million and sell for $30 million. Simple deal, quick profit, bye-bye and thank you very much.'

'When you say "quickly", how quick is that?'

'I buy and sell at the same time. Immediate profit.'

'So, your onward sale should have happened as soon as you bought the yacht, back-to-back?' Polk asked.

'Yes, back-to-back, same time.'

'I see, and what actually happened?'

'The guy buying from me pulled out. When I asked my lawyers to sue him, they said he can walk away from our contract. I said, "You're joking—either you're wrong about that, or you've made a big mistake with my contracts." Then they refused to advise me any more! So, my lawyers create this big problem and then do nothing to fix it.'

'From what you have told me, Mr Berzin, this seems to be clear negligence in the drafting of your contracts. We will obviously need to see the relevant papers, and discuss this in more detail, but I expect to send a strong letter of claim to Davis & Hendry. We will do our very best to recover most, if not all, of your losses.'

* * *

Malcolm Connell read the letter of claim and sighed. As Davis & Hendry's risk management partner, Malcolm had been expecting a claim ever since he heard about the call from Berzin three weeks earlier. The letter read:

In breach of your firm's duty to ensure our client's contracts were drafted back-to-back, the terms of the onward sale contract allow the ultimate purchaser to withdraw from the deal, while our client still remains legally bound to buy the yacht. As a result of your negligence, our client has lost the chance to make a guaranteed profit of $12 million.

Unless your client agrees to compensate our client in full within fourteen days, our client will bring legal action against your firm to recover his losses, together with costs and interest.

Meanwhile, please provide a copy of your client files by return.

Malcolm knew he had to provide a copy of the firm's files to Polk, who would then search for further ammunition to support Berzin's claim.

When I read the letter, I shared Malcolm's pessimism, though our task was to build the firm's defence. This meant asking exactly what Berzin had instructed Davis & Hendry to do; what precisely was their duty? Had Berzin made it clear the contracts must be back-to-back and that his onward sale would fund his initial purchase? Had he reviewed and approved the contracts? Even if this was an error, had it actually caused a loss or would the ultimate buyer have withdrawn in any event?

There were various potential defences but the starting point was challenging.

* * *

I arrived at the offices of Davis & Hendry and their receptionist showed me into the boardroom. As Malcolm entered the room, we exchanged pleasantries and then began a series of interviews with the lawyers who had prepared Berzin's contracts.

We first met the head of the firm's commercial department, John Olde, who was on record as the client supervising partner. A burly man with a powerful stare, Olde acknowledged his position of responsibility but duly explained why this mess had nothing to do with him.

Olde explained that as this work had come to the firm through Michael Wright, an experienced consultant attorney, Olde's own involvement had been 'purely high level'. We needed to speak to Michael.

Michael greeted us with a forced smile. I explained that I was representing Davis & Hendry and its insurers, and we needed to know more about this transaction and the drafting of the contracts. Michael nodded and began his explanation.

'I was introduced to Mr Berzin at a charity dinner a few years ago by another client who knew Berzin's wife. We stayed in touch. He called me last year to ask for my help in buying a superyacht. He wanted me to draft the purchase contract. These deals are usually a mad rush, but here there was only one complicating factor.'

'What was that?'

'The yacht had been damaged in an accident a few weeks earlier. It was not seaworthy, and the repairs were due to take another five months. Berzin used this point to his advantage by negotiating a reduced price of $18 million, conditional upon the repairs being completed by a longstop date.'

'So, you addressed the risk that the repairs would drag on for longer?' I asked.

'Yes, I drafted a conditional contract between the yacht owner and Berzin's company, Bluewaves Ltd. If the repairs were not completed within five months, Berzin could walk away. But if the repairs were done by the longstop date, Bluewaves would become obliged to complete the contract and pay for the yacht within the following month.'

'So, there was a two-stage process: a longstop date for the repairs, then one month for payment and completion?'

'Correct. That was our way of protecting Berzin's position, and the purchase contract achieved its purpose,' Michael explained. 'The only problem is with the onward sale—the flip contract.'

'Tell us about that, please. When did Mr Berzin first contact you about an onward sale?'

'Berzin called me around two months before the repair longstop date. He had found a buyer willing to pay $12 million more than his purchase price, which was obviously a great deal. The buyer was the media mogul David Handsome. Handsome was prepared to complete the flip contract at the same time as the purchase contract, which meant Berzin could use the money from Handsome to fund his own purchase. Honestly, it couldn't have been simpler,' Michael said. 'Berzin should have made a $12 million profit, no question.'

'So, you then drafted the flip contract to sell the yacht on to Handsome?'

'Not personally, no. Our firm drafted the flip contract, but I didn't do it myself. You see, the onward sale was structured as a sale of Bluewaves rather than a sale of the yacht itself.'

'I see, but why does that mean you didn't draft the flip contract?' I asked.

'Our firm is very specialized. I advise on commercial contracts for the sale of tangible assets like the yacht. Our corporate department handles the sale of companies. In this case, Susan Dakin, one of our corporate lawyers, drafted the flip contract for the sale of Bluewaves to Handsome. You'll need to speak to Susan about why the contracts didn't match up.'

'Yes, we will be speaking to Susan shortly, but did you also remain involved?'

'A little, but purely at a high level.'

* * *

Malcolm and I reflected on Michael's explanations and then we met Susan Dakin, who was evidently concerned. I thanked Susan for meeting with us and asked her to explain the background, as she saw it.

'I remember taking a call from Michael, who told me Mr Berzin wanted to sell one of his companies that was about to buy a superyacht. He asked me to draft the flip contract. Michael sent me a copy of the purchase contract, and we had a brief chat. I then had a call with Mr Berzin, who lives abroad. It seemed simple and, of course, Michael would still review the draft flip contract.'

'So, you were dealing with Mr Berzin directly but running things past Michael?' I asked.

'Yes.'

Once Susan had confirmed the nature of the transactions, I asked her about the drafting of the flip contract and her thoughts on the letter of claim.

'Unfortunately, I think we have a real problem. There is a gap in the completion provisions in the two contracts. I did what I thought was required—I used the same longstop date as in the purchase contract. But looking at it again now, the conditionality is slightly different, and Handsome has exploited that at Mr Berzin's expense.'

'Can you talk us through that?' I asked.

'The longstop date in the flip contract isn't actually linked to the completion of the repairs—it's linked to the completion of the purchase contract itself, which will happen up to one month later. This mismatch creates a timing gap.'

'And how did that work out in practice?'

'The longstop date in the purchase contract was met, so Bluewaves became obliged to complete the purchase contract within the following month. But Handsome could still walk away from the flip contract, since the longstop date in the flip contract had not been met—Bluewaves had not yet bought the yacht.'

'I see.'

'Handsome has used the mismatch to pull out of the deal,' Susan added. 'Perhaps he could no longer afford to pay, or he realized the price was too high. Either way, Berzin is stuck because he is legally bound to buy the yacht through Bluewaves, even though his funding has apparently fallen through.'

'I see the difficulty, thank you for explaining that,' I said. 'Returning to the drafting stage, though, did you advise Mr Berzin about the completion provisions in the flip contract and send him a draft for his approval?'

'I sent him the draft, which he approved, but as far as I remember we never advised on this point. I relied on Michael to cross-reference these details and make sure the contracts matched up properly, but it seems that ultimately they didn't.'

* * *

Through his lawsuit against Davis & Hendry, Berzin eventually secured a settlement payment from the firm's insurers, albeit in the sum of $3 million rather than the $12 million he had claimed.

Davis & Hendry negotiated this lower sum because they had a viable causation defence to the claim. It had emerged that Handsome would never have been able to pay the $30 million price even if the longstop date had been met, so Berzin arguably would have faced the same funding gap even if the contracts had been drafted correctly.

Nonetheless, the firm had to pay its insurance deductible towards the settlement. There were also personal costs: Michael fell into a depression and Susan left the firm six months later 'by mutual consent'.

Olde survived, although as a diminished force because his partners were annoyed at the cost and reputational damage caused by the claim, and dismayed by his involvement having been 'purely high level'.

Lessons

This case is a prime example of how a genuine client problem, in this case the loss of a contractual right, can lead to a lawsuit against the client's professional advisors. It also illustrates the small details and fine margins that can have very serious unintended consequences.

Aside from the risks involved in having light-touch supervision, what warnings might have put Michael and Susan on alert that this was a risky transaction from a potential liability perspective?

Handover and divisions of responsibility

An internal division of responsibility, and especially a handover from one department to another, is a common cause of problems.

Is the briefing clear and comprehensive? Is everyone agreed about the degree of overlap between individuals and departments? Who has final responsibility for key documents?

Clarity is especially important where multiple international offices are involved in the same matter.

Back-to-back contracts

In the legal sphere, back-to-back contracts present a particular risk as any mismatch could have a significant consequence for the client. This risk is magnified where the client is relying on receivables due under one contract to fund liabilities payable under another.

Lack of information from the client

In this case, both advisors were unclear about the client's funding plans which, if clarified, might have improved their focus during the drafting process. By focusing more closely upon the funding gap, they may have been more likely to spot the subsequent mismatch in the completion provisions.

CHAPTER 2

'HEALTH WARNING'

'I don't agree with this; it's all wrong.'

Robin looked at me with dark eyes. His hair was greyer than when I first met him, two years ago, and his voice sounded tired.

'The claim is a try-on,' he added. 'It always has been.'

Robin's law firm and its insurers were on the verge of paying out several million pounds to a wheeler-dealer. And it was simply not fair.

'As I keep saying, I'm sure I advised Derek about this point. He's made millions out of this deal and, now the market has crashed, we're the scapegoats.'

Robin had served Derek as his real estate lawyer for two decades. They first met when Derek was an aspiring property developer and Robin was a rising star at a leading law firm. They complemented each other: the risk-taker and the safe pair of hands.

Fast-forward thirteen years to the height of the property boom, by which time Derek's real estate empire had made him a multimillionaire, at least on paper.

Derek was considering buying a condominium complex he thought was undervalued. The freehold owners had granted a ninety-nine-year head lease to their subsidiary company, which sublet units to each of the residents. The head lease was on the market for £22 million, and Derek had driven the price down to £20 million.

The only snag was the seller insisted on completing the sale by the end of its financial year, in a fortnight's time. That was a fraction of the usual timescale for a major property deal. It risked rushing the documentation and skimping on the due diligence. But Derek told Robin to get on with it. This was the 'deal of the century' and a firm like Robin's should move quickly. Who was Robin to disagree?

The next two weeks flew by. First, Robin ensured the seller's lawyer provided a certificate of title; a warranty that no title defect was evident on the face of the head lease. This would allow Robin to concentrate on other aspects of the transaction, given the tight timescale.

Derek was not interested in the legal 'niceties', but Robin insisted he make time for a meeting. The weekend before completion, Robin visited Derek and brought the draft loan agreements, a site plan and the head lease. He spread them out on the table and talked Derek through the key terms of each document. Robin focused on three key aspects of the deal: what was being transferred, how it was being financed and the lack of due diligence, which made Robin uneasy. Derek said:

'Robin, relax, this will all be fine. It's the deal of the century, and all I need you to do is make sure it completes on time.'

After the meeting, Robin emailed Derek with these last words of caution:

Dear Derek,

Health warning

Further to our discussion at your house last weekend, the financing and transfer agreements are all ready for signature. However, I must reiterate my concerns about the inevitable lack of due diligence on this acquisition, which is a consequence of the extremely tight timescale.

I have done my best to review the relevant documentation and consider the legal issues, but I cannot be responsible if an unexpected problem emerges that it has not been possible for me to identify within this timescale.

I raised these concerns with you last weekend, but you are determined to proceed despite the limited due diligence.

Yours …

The 'deal of the century' completed on time.

* * *

Over the following years, the value of the property grew and Derek continued to build his portfolio. Derek was riding high, and Robin was his trusted advisor.

Eventually, Derek decided to sell the property to a pension fund for £36 million. However, the buyer's lawyer identified what they considered to be a defect in the head lease. Although they did not dispute Derek's ownership of the property, they said one term in the head lease was a blight on the land. That term permitted the freeholder to move the swimming pool and other amenities away from the beach side to the road side of the complex. They acknowledged that the freeholder would be foolish to do so, but it was possible. The buyer reduced its offer by £6 million, saying 'Deal or no deal?'

Derek was furious. Who did these pension guys think they were, inventing problems to justify a derisory offer? Derek was sure this 'problem' would never materialize—indeed, if it really was a defect, how could he have borrowed so much money using the land as security?

But when Derek found other interested buyers, they raised the same concern and each offered £6 million less than his asking price. Meanwhile, the problem was compounded by a falling property market.

Derek contacted the freeholder to see if they would resolve the issue by amending the head lease. They agreed, but only at a price of £6 million.

Derek called Robin:

'Rob, I don't like to do this to you. You've been my eyes and ears, you've helped me for over twenty years, and you've been the best lawyer in the business. But, Rob … I have no choice. There's a problem with the legals here. I'm losing £6 million. I've got to bring a claim on your insurance.'

* * *

When I first interviewed Robin, in my role as defence counsel to his firm, he had a clear recollection of having met with Derek prior to completion, raising concerns about the limited due diligence, and sending his 'health warning' email. Robin believed that he and Derek had discussed the main provisions of the head lease, including the clause in question. Robin thought he had explained the term to Derek, who was unconcerned because the freeholder would never move the swimming pool away from the beach.

Would Robin's recollection of his discussions with Derek provide a defence to the lawsuit? Not necessarily. As the litigation progressed, Derek's sworn evidence was different: he said Robin had not raised this point at all. Indeed, Derek said if Robin *had* raised the issue, Derek would either have negotiated a price reduction or walked away from the deal.

Unless Robin was able to support his defence with documentary evidence of the advice given, the court would probably give Derek the benefit of any doubt. Regrettably, Robin had no file note of his advice.

Could Robin rely on the certificate of title to pass any liability on to the seller? No, because the problem was the commercial impact of the clause on the land value rather than a pure defect in ownership rights.

Surely Robin's 'health warning' email would provide a defence to the claim? After all, he had made it plain to Derek that this was a rush job and issues might be missed. Yes and no. The email helped, because it showed the constraints under which Robin had been operating. However, the alleged negligence related to a document Robin had in fact reviewed, so the problem was not actually caused by the limited due diligence.

Robin understood the logic of this advice, and the risk of losing at trial, but he kept returning to the unfairness of the situation.

'As I say, I'm sure Derek was content with the head lease, so he's just trying to see what he can recover from our insurers — and they're playing into his hands by giving credence to his false evidence.'

Robin's frustration was palpable and deeply felt. However, although his firm and its insurers had defended the case thus far, they could not risk going to trial without specific documentary evidence to support their defence. Galling as it was for Robin, the claim had to be settled.

Derek recovered almost £4 million, representing two-thirds of his claimed loss. The insurers paid most of this sum but Robin's firm had to contribute its insurance deductible of £200,000.

The wider costs of the claim were much greater:

- around 150 hours of lost chargeable time during the litigation;

- an increase in the firm's annual insurance premium;

- a broken client relationship;

- reputational damage from press reports; and

- stress for Robin and his family.

Lessons

Robin was alert to several warning signs or 'red flags': the tight timescales, the resulting lack of due diligence and Derek's disinterest in the legal issues.

Robin tried to protect himself by:

- insisting on a face-to-face meeting with Derek;

- explaining the key terms of the deal;

- ensuring the seller's lawyer gave a certificate of title; and

- sending his 'health warning' email.

Those were sensible steps, but other factors turned out to be even more crucial:

- Robin proceeded to advise on the terms of the head lease despite obtaining the certificate of title and without any recorded limitations to the scope of his duty, thereby opening himself up to broader duties than were strictly necessary;

- Robin did not take or retain notes of his advice and Derek's instructions—perhaps the familiarity of his close long-term, working relationship with Derek led Robin to take fewer precautions than normal; and

- Robin's 'health warning' email was too general. As he had advised on the terms of the head lease, and Derek had confirmed they were commercially acceptable, he should have recorded that specific point.

CHAPTER 3

WHO DROPPED THE BILLION-DOLLAR BALL?

'Ding out! Ding out!' the fans chanted beside the entrance to the Tigers' stadium on the outskirts of the sprawling city.

Inside, the club's chief executive, Adam Thomson, spoke on live television:

'I have a message for all our loyal supporters: we will not allow our ownership dispute with Mr Ding to hurt the team's performance, our fans' pride or the financial stability of the club. We are all fully committed to winning the championship.'

Thomson left the press conference, with cameras flashing in his face as he walked past the players' changing rooms, up the stairs and into the boardroom.

'Well done, Adam,' said Dick Meadows, his fellow director and a Tigers legend, 'but we need to sort this out.'

'You're right, but there's a lot of money at stake, the kind of money that could mean our families never need to work again. We've got to make the most of this opportunity.'

'Opportunity?' Dick said. 'Windfall, more like. We haven't done anything to deserve this kind of money, and it's not ours by right.'

'This isn't about ethics, Dick; the contract says what it says and the fans are on our side. Anyway, the board has already resolved to hold out for the extra billion. If Ding doesn't pay by Friday, we'll sue him.'

* * *

Flanked by an aide and two bodyguards, Ding waited in the tenth-floor lobby of Ebdon Selby, the city's premier law firm.

'Mr Ding, I'm so sorry to have kept you waiting,' said Francis Starr, the firm's head of litigation, as he strode confidently across the room. 'It's a pleasure to meet you,' Francis added as he shook Ding's hand. 'Please, follow me.'

They entered the boardroom and, after some pleasantries, Francis said:

'Mr Ding, you're a busy man, so I'll get straight to the point. I understand you bought a minority stake in the Tigers and agreed to buy the remaining shares from their management team five years later—that is, now. You've refused to pay the price that the management are demanding, so they have sued you. Is that right?'

Francis looked at Ding, expecting his answer, but Ding said nothing. After an awkward silence, Ding's aide said:

'The venerable chairman asks that you direct your questions to me, Mr Starr. My name is Yang and I am Mr Ding's spokesman. Yes, you are correct that Mr Ding remains willing to buy the management's stake—he very much wants to own the Tigers, outright. He is an honourable man, and he has the means to pay their price. But why should he? What can you do about this, Mr Starr?'

'Well, from my initial review of the contract, the starting point is difficult,' Francis said. 'The pricing formula is clear, and it produces the price the management team are demanding. But before I suggest how to tackle this, can you confirm when Mr Ding first became aware of the issue?'

'Actually, one of our internal audit team noticed it only a few months after the contract was signed, five years ago,' Mr Yang said. 'We did nothing at that stage, because we thought the management team wouldn't spot the mistake or, even if they did, they would never try to enforce it. I mean, it produces a ridiculous figure.'

'I see, thank you for explaining that,' Francis said. 'At this early stage, I can see two possible ways out of this, though neither will be easy. The first is to defend the management's claim by seeking rectification of the contract. This means asking the court to rule that the formula contains a mistake that the court needs to correct. However, rectification claims can be hard to establish.'

'What is the second option?'

'If Mr Ding ultimately has to pay more than intended, he may be able to recover the difference by suing the professional firms who advised him on the terms of the contract. In that case, we would need to bring any claim before the limitation period expires, in March next year.'

'I see,' replied Mr Yang. 'I like your suggestions. Our lawyers drafted the main body of the contract, but not the pricing formula; the first draft was prepared by our internal investment bankers, and we then ran it past our accountants, Hartsons.'

'Right, in that case, please send me all of your documents from that drafting process, in order for me to advise you on the potential for a claim against Hartsons.'

Francis Starr received Mr Yang's files and his associate reviewed the documents and confirmed that the draft pricing formula for the second tranche had indeed been passed to Hartsons shortly before the contract was signed. However, there was one difference between the draft formula sent to Hartsons and the final version in the signed contract—and that amendment seemed to have caused the present dispute.

Mr Yang duly instructed Francis to write a letter of claim threatening legal action against Hartsons.

* * *

How does it feel to be accused of making a billion-dollar mistake?

That was Gemma Dickson's fate as she contemplated the letter of claim received by Hartsons.

Gemma's career had progressed seamlessly through the ranks to her present position as a partner in the firm. Gemma's intelligence, hard work and determination had earned her great success. However, this claim now threatened the very *existence* of Hartsons, as the headline figure exceeded the firm's insurance coverage by more than $500 million.

Gemma greeted me with a firm handshake but she avoided meeting my eyes. I introduced myself as Hartsons' defence counsel and confirmed that I had reviewed the firm's client files ahead of our meeting. After some pleasantries, I asked Gemma about the background to the deal.

'It dominated my life for about three months,' Gemma said. 'The club was owned by a management team of former players. Although the management needed outside investment, they didn't want to sell "their" club just yet. I think they were torn between their love of the club and the amount of money they could make by selling their shares.'

'What happened?'

'The compromise was that Mr Ding's takeover would be in two stages. He would buy 49 per cent of the shares immediately—tranche one—and then the remaining 51 per cent five years later—tranche two.'

'Did you deal with Mr Ding himself?'

'No, I took instructions from his right-hand man, Mr Yang, who was based in Hong Kong. I never met him either, but we emailed and spoke by telephone. The deal was driven from Hong Kong.'

'So, the deal structure was in place and Mr Ding bought his first tranche minority stake,' I said. 'Tell me about the pricing formula for the second tranche.'

'The price of the second tranche was a multiple of the club's aggregate profits over the five-year period. So, if the profits were $20 million and the multiplier was five, the price would be $100 million. The basic idea was simple.'

'I can see, from your file,' I said, 'that Mr Yang sent you the draft formula a few days before the parties signed the contract, but the final version was slightly different. The file shows a handwritten amendment to the formula, changing the word 'including' to 'excluding', in relation to whether transfer dealings were factored into the pricing calculation. The amendment seems to have been typed up and included in the final contract. Is the handwriting yours, Gemma?'

'Yes, it's my writing, but I would only have made the amendment on client instructions.'

'Can you talk me through the significance of the amendment?'

'It changed the definition of aggregate profits, to exclude the club's transfer dealings—buying and selling players. Excluding transfer dealings can either increase or decrease the profits, depending on whether the club spends more on new players than it receives from player sales.'

'Yes,' I said, 'and in this case, it seems to have had a dramatic impact. According to the letter of claim, the club spent about $200 million more than it received, over the five-year period. The problem for Mr Ding is that the pricing formula takes no account of those transfer expenses, so the profit figure is much higher than if transfer dealings were included within the profit calculations. The five-fold multiplier then exaggerates the problem: it turns the $200 million increase into $1 billion more than if transfer dealings had been included.'

'Yes, the amendment does seem to have worked against Mr Ding, but that is just because the club went on a spending spree. If the club had been a net seller of players, the formula would have worked in Mr Ding's favour.'

'That makes sense, and we'll certainly explore that line of defence. Meanwhile, though, do you actually remember having made the amendment?' I asked.

'To be honest, I can't. But it was a commercial matter so, as I say, I must have made it based on client instructions. I mean, pricing is always a commercial issue for the client, isn't it?' Gemma said, looking straight at me.

'Yes, pricing is a commercial issue, though we also need to address the specific allegation that this amendment was made in error—how do you respond to that?'

'That's nonsense. I wouldn't have made the amendment unless Mr Yang had instructed me to make it.'

'So, are you saying that Mr Yang instructed you to make the amendment?'

'I'm saying that he must have instructed me,' Gemma said, 'because otherwise I wouldn't have done it.'

'Just to be clear, does that mean you don't actually remember Mr Yang having instructed you, but you're sure he must have done so?'

'Exactly. I can't remember every detail of every deal, but I'm sure this would have come from Mr Yang.'

'I understand, but the difficulty is there is nothing on the file that records those instructions.'

'We must have dealt with it by phone. You can see that I made this amendment the day before signing. That's always a hectic time. Most of our work on this deal involved heavy due diligence, rather than dealing with this formula,' Gemma said. 'It's certainly my normal practice to take notes— you'll have seen many on the file—but I can't be expected to do it every single time.'

'Yes, I understand.' I said, before pausing for a moment. 'I appreciate the pressure you were under, Gemma, and the difficulty of this situation. I do need to play devil's advocate, though, and ask why you think Mr Yang would have asked you to make this change?'

'There could have been any number of reasons, but I can't recall if he ever explained it.'

'Assuming, for a moment, that Mr Yang instructed you to make this amendment but without explaining the reasons, what would have happened next?' I asked. 'Do you think you advised him about it?'

'Probably not. The file doesn't show that he requested advice so it must have been an instruction, pure and simple. Unless he had asked for my advice, I would not have second-guessed what he told me about the commercial agreement on price.'

'I see, and I can appreciate that. But the difficulty is that in Mr Yang's initial email, he said he was 'running the formula past you'. I know that is a vague phrase, but I haven't seen any response saying you were not actually advising on the formula.'

'The files aren't perfect,' Gemma said, 'but we were up against a deadline, and I'm sure I would have made that point clear when we spoke by phone.'

'Right, I see, thank you. For now, I just have one further question for you, Gemma. Mr Ding's lawyers also say that you should have done sample calculations to show the impact of the amendment in various scenarios, as a sense-check. With hindsight, do you think ...'

'No, as I say, this was a commercial matter, and I followed what the client wanted.'

* * *

Once the interview process was completed, we responded to Francis Starr's letter of claim. Francis was undeterred by Hartsons' defences but he agreed Ding should not litigate against Hartsons until he had exhausted all other options; here, his rectification defence against the club's management. If Ding's rectification defence succeeded, he would have no liability to pay the extra billion to the management, and no need to sue Hartsons.

Francis's only concern was that time was running short for Ding to bring any such claim against Hartsons, should that prove necessary. To preserve Ding's legal rights, Francis proposed a 'standstill' of the limitation deadline for one year while the rectification proceedings took their course. Hartsons gladly agreed.

* * *

The rectification proceedings rumbled along until the court reached its verdict: rectification was refused and Ding had to pay the extra billion dollars.

Hartsons was once again in the firing line, but just as Francis Starr was preparing to issue court proceedings, his associate burst in and said:

'Francis, we have a problem—the standstill agreement expired three weeks ago, and it looks like we forgot to extend it, so Ding is out of time for bringing this claim!'

Ding's claim against Hartsons was indeed time-barred, and so ultimately it was Francis Starr who dropped the billion-dollar ball.

Lessons

In some ways, this was a typically challenging transaction for the professional advisor: drafting under pressure, taking instructions from a distant client and being at least one step removed from the commercial negotiations. But were there warning signs that could have helped Gemma to steer a safer course? And what about Francis and the missed limitation date?

Unclear scope of Hartsons' retainer

Even assuming that Mr Yang instructed Gemma to make the drafting amendment, it was unsafe for her to *assume* that he did not require her advice. Was the pricing formula *purely* a commercial matter that was beyond the scope of Hartsons' duty? Probably not, unless the scope of their engagement was expressly limited. Otherwise, there would have been little purpose in Mr Yang obtaining accountancy input on the pricing formula.

Amending a crucial term in a contract

Pricing is always a key issue that requires extra care. It would have been prudent of Gemma to have done a test calculation using sample numbers, as a sense-check. She would then have identified the potentially massive adverse consequences of making this amendment. Had she done so, Gemma would doubtless have drawn those risks to Mr Yang's attention, while making it clear that she was not giving commercial advice. Gemma should have asked Mr Yang to consider the issue and confirm Mr Ding's instructions.

Instructions by telephone but no notes

Gemma's lack of file notes could have seriously undermined her firm's defence. This is a regrettably common difficulty for defendant firms.

Deadline disaster

Why did Francis and his associate miss the limitation deadline? Did they each rely upon the other or was it simply in neither advisor's diary? Even the biggest and best firms can make such basic oversights, despite widespread usage of electronic diary systems.

The costs can be substantial; in this case, the missed deadline was worth up to $1 billion for Francis's firm and its insurers, as Ding would invariably have proceeded to sue them for having jeopardized his recovery claim against Hartsons. Even in more typical cases, the costs are substantial and there is broader damage to the firm's reputation and client relationships.

CHAPTER 4

FROM CLIENT TO CLAIMANT?

Why might a client sue your firm even though they value your advice and have no desire to cause you trouble?

In other words, why might a client become a claimant?

The legalistic answer is that your client may believe they can establish the elements of a liability claim against your firm. Typically, they would be acting upon independent legal advice that you failed to act with reasonable skill and care and your alleged breach of duty has caused them to suffer recoverable loss.

However, the practical answer is that your client faces a major problem, worth a lot of money, and there is a prospect of recovering at least some of it from your firm and its insurers.

Client problems often arise long after any alleged mistake was made; they 'blow up' as if from nowhere. We have already seen an example of such a problem in Chapter 2; Derek's difficulty was that he could only sell his property for much less than it should have been worth, and this problem emerged years after professional advice was given.

Three major problems a client could face

Although the range of potential client problems is broad, claims commonly arise where a client:

- has acquired a defective asset;

- faces a demand from a third party; or

- loses a valuable right.

1. Your client has acquired a defective asset

Your client may have acquired an asset that turns out to be less valuable than expected. Whatever the asset, and whatever your profession, you may find yourself in the firing line if your client tries to recoup the 'lost' value.

The asset could be tangible, such as a property that has lost value as a result of an alleged title or ownership defect. The client may allege you should have spotted the defect and warned them about it, in which case they would either have (i) insisted the defect be cured before they bought the asset or (ii) simply never bought it.

Whether the claim is genuine or spurious may only be determined at trial. Meanwhile, your firm would face the costs of defending the litigation and this would bring pressure to make a settlement payment.

Sometimes the problem arises from a defect in the quality of an asset. This is common in construction projects; even a cutting-edge building could be riddled with latent defects. The problems might only emerge years later but, when they do, the architects, contractors and project managers invariably become deep-pocket defendants.

In some cases, defects may be apparent from an early stage, such as in the construction of the new Wembley Stadium in London. The Wembley construction project ran £300 million over budget and resulted in a £253 million claim by the prime contractor against the design engineers, involving allegations that their steelworks design could never have been built within the agreed costs plan. The litigation was eventually settled on confidential terms, but only once the legal costs had reportedly reached around £30 million.

Liability claims also arise where a client's asset is intangible, such as shares in a business. The value of the business might prove much lower than the buyer (your client) thought. Such a problem could arise from:

- a legal issue – for example, the value of a business will be reduced if its intellectual property rights are defective;

- an accountancy issue – for instance, if it emerges that the acquisition price was based upon dubious accounting assumptions, this will reduce the current share price; or

- a valuation issue – for instance, if the assets of a business are overvalued, a subsequent correction in its financial statements could hurt your client as the current owner.

In each case, the spotlight falls on the due diligence conducted by the lawyers, accountants and other advisors. Did they miss something or are they being made the fall guys for their client's poor bargain?

Another common problem is faced by banks whose loans are secured over properties that turn out to be worth only a fraction of the purchase price. The bank's asset (its security interest) becomes practically worthless because it covers little of the borrower's outstanding debt. Typically, the bank sues each of the professional advisors involved:

- surveyors are accused of over-valuing the property;

- accountants are alleged to have misstated the borrower's financial status; and

- if there is any hint of mortgage fraud, the conveyancing lawyers may face accusations of being involved in the fraud.

In each case, there is invariably a dispute about whether the bank's claims are justified or if its losses were self-inflicted through its own reckless lending practices.

2. Your client faces a demand from a third party

Your client will have a problem if they ever face a demand from a third party to pay a sum much greater than they expected.

This usually generates a battle between the client and the third party about whether the demand is payable. But if the demand *is* payable, or even if there is a real risk that it might be, the next dispute is between the client and their advisor(s) about who is to blame. The client will say:

'I deny any liability to pay this inflated demand, but if I am liable to pay, then it is your fault and you must compensate me.'

Such problems may arise from drafting errors in documents that create legal rights, although the client's lawyers are not necessarily the only defendants, especially where other advisors also held the drafting pen.

Likewise, a demand may be made by a regulatory authority, perhaps to the surprise of the client. For example, liability claims can result from demands made by tax authorities. Imagine your client is a corporation that requires complex tax-planning strategies. You advised about how to mitigate their tax liability, but years later the tax authorities scrutinize your client's affairs and make a demand for unpaid taxes running into the millions. Your client denies liability but, if they must pay, they may look to your firm for compensation.

3. Your client loses a valuable right

If your client cannot enforce their intended rights, the blame game will begin.

For example, a client might lose a right to exercise an option, enforce a contract or bring a legal action.

A client may be a victim of fraud, perhaps even to the degree that a client company becomes insolvent and goes into liquidation after its assets have been stolen. In that scenario, the liquidators must consider pursuing legal claims against third parties, including the company's former professional advisors, for the benefit of its creditors. A typical defendant is the company's former auditors, whom the liquidators may blame for having issued clean audit reports rather than identifying any 'red flags' that could have revealed the fraud.

Likewise, a significant problem may arise if a client loses insurance coverage for a liability or loss. In Chapter 7, we will see an example of a client suing an insurance broker because the client's product recall losses were uninsured. Although that was a scapegoat claim, there are also legitimate claims against brokers where their client turns out to be uninsured, or underinsured, against a specified risk. Rightly or wrongly, the broker is the obvious target.

We have also seen, in the previous subsection, how tax authority investigations might lead to a demand for your client to pay back-taxes. However, regulatory investigations may be much broader; for example, potentially leading to the closure of an entire business or product line if it appears to have fallen foul of the rules. Sometimes alleged infractions remain undetected for years. Regardless of the outcome, a client's costs of merely responding to the investigation can amount to millions. If the outcome is adverse, the client will face massive financial, regulatory and reputational harm.

Will the client simply accept this as a fact of life or sue the advisors who helped them navigate the regulatory minefield?

The key to understanding why a client might sue your firm lies in seeing matters from their perspective as well as your own. This means anticipating problems that your clients could face and the resulting risks for you and your firm.

CHAPTER 5

FOUR KINDS OF CLAIMANT

H ow do clients respond to major problems such as those outlined in the previous chapter?

Although they may seek to resolve the problem commercially, that may be impossible or the costs of any resolution could still leave the client with large losses. Simple resolutions are the exception rather than the rule.

Rather, there are four typical client reactions that lead to a lawsuit against the client's professional advisors.

1. The Reluctant Claimant

Many present or former clients are reluctant to bring a claim against their advisors. However, this will not deter them from suing if they have suffered a loss that they consider to be your fault.

The Reluctant Claimant may even be compelled to bring a claim. For instance, company directors are duty-bound to act in the best interests of their company, which could involve bringing a claim against its advisors. When the directors evaluate their prospects of success, the threshold is low as 'success' will include even a modest settlement payment. This is often achievable, even if the claim is far from clear-cut. Indeed, a lack of documentary evidence often works in the claimant's favour, as it tends to hamper the advisor's defence.

The Reluctant Claimant may also take comfort from the fact that, as they see it, they are really suing your firm's insurers. But this is only partly true, as many of the costs would rest with you and your firm: lost billable hours, wasted management time, your firm's insurance deductible, reputational damage and all of the personal stress. Moreover, a poor claims record would also lead to increases in your firm's annual professional indemnity insurance premium.

2. The Ice-Cold Claimant

The Ice-Cold Claimant sees matters in black and white:

- they have suffered a loss;

- they are sure it is your fault; and

- suing you is a regrettable fact of commercial life.

Even if the Ice-Cold Claimant is one of your current clients, they will instruct lawyers to pursue the claim against you robustly. Those lawyers will scrutinize your client files, looking for evidence to support the claim.

However, the Ice-Cold Claimant focuses on the real issues and:

- they have no interest in creating publicity, twisting facts or pursuing the claim for tactical reasons;

- they will be open to resolving the claim through a reasonable settlement; and

- they may instruct you again in the future, if they retain confidence in your ability.

3. The Indignant Victim

The Indignant Victim reacts to their problem emotionally in distress and anger. They may have good reason for their indignation; perhaps they have lost a large sum of money through no fault of their own.

Provided they keep a sense of perspective and control over their emotions, the Indignant Victim is a formidable claimant: credible, sincere and compelling.

However, if they lose their sense of perspective, they are liable to act unpredictably: to refuse reasonable settlement offers, continue with the claim for vindication rather than compensation, or go to the press.

4. The Opportunist

Although the Opportunist may face a genuine problem, they also spy a chance to extract cash from your firm and its insurers.

They may invent, distort or suppress evidence to support their claim. Over time, they may even come to believe that their version of events is the absolute truth.

The galling thing is that even if the claim is dubious, it might be hard to defend. Even where you gave the correct advice, you could face difficulties if the events happened years ago and there are gaps in your files. This concern is addressed further in Chapters 6 and 7 in the context of preventing scapegoat claims.

CHAPTER 6

SCAPEGOAT CLAIMS

Where a client faces a major problem evidently caused by their advisor's mistake, it is only natural for them to sue. Liability may seem like a foregone conclusion.

However, matters are rarely that simple because there is often genuine doubt about what caused the client's problem. Despite this, the client may press ahead with a lawsuit to obtain a big-money settlement. They are spurred on by the potential to recoup their alleged losses, in some cases represented by lawyers acting on a 'no win, no fee' basis such that there is little financial risk in the client pursuing the claim. Therefore, a client's problem could draw you into litigation even though you are not at fault.

There could be at least four other causes of the client's problem:

- an error by a third party such as another professional advisor to the client;

- an error by the client themselves;

- a misjudgement or poor bargain by the client; or

- misfortune that was nobody's fault.

The true cause of the client's problem may not be established until trial if the claim progresses that far without being settled.

Meanwhile:

- you would have to spend valuable time and money investigating and defending the claim: working with defence counsel, providing discovery documents and giving witness evidence;

- you could face practical and evidential difficulties in establishing your defence; and

- you already feel targeted as a scapegoat.

Mounting costs and the acute risk of damage to your firm's reputation create pressure to make a settlement payment.

> This is the scapegoat threat: the spectre of being sued by a client even though you gave the right advice.

* * *

Where the client has engaged several professional advisors, they may each become a defendant. This can happen if the client sues each advisor or where the client sues one firm that, in turn, sues others for a contribution towards any damages that may be awarded.

The client may not care who exactly is to blame, so long as some or all of the defendants pay towards a global settlement or fight it out among themselves at trial. If the liability truly is shared between several professionals, then this is damaging but not unfair. Likewise, if a firm and its client are each partly to blame, the courts will reduce the size of any damages award to reflect the client's 'contributory negligence'.

However, for each firm that is not even partly to blame, the lawsuit represents a scapegoat claim.

For instance, imagine that a client's building has serious defects in construction. The architects, contractor and project manager could all become deep-pocket defendants. If the client's problem was caused by:

- defective design, then the architects may be at fault but the contractor and project manager are at risk of being scapegoats;

- defective workmanship, then the contractor may be at fault whereas the architects and project manager are at risk of being scapegoats; or

- poor supervision and planning, then the project manager (and perhaps the contractor) may be at fault but the architects are at risk of being scapegoats.

* * *

Is it not simple to defend such a scapegoat claim?

Only if the legal and factual issues are straightforward and there is strong documentary evidence to support the advisor's defence.

However, that is rarely the case because issues of liability are usually complex and the documentary evidence may be incomplete. Each defendant will be put to vast expense to investigate and respond to the claim, long before any finding of liability. As we saw in Chapter 2, Robin's lack of documentary evidence meant his firm was drawn into costly litigation that was settled shortly before trial.

This scapegoat threat means no advisor may safely assume they can stay out of trouble simply by being careful and avoiding major errors. Claims also arise from *clients'* mistakes, misjudgements and misfortune.

CHAPTER 7

PREVENTING
SCAPEGOAT CLAIMS

B y its very nature, a scapegoat claim arises from a problem that you did not cause or control.

Nonetheless, you can reduce the likelihood of facing a scapegoat claim by acting on warning signs that may arise within your clients' actions and your work for them.

This chapter addresses four risk factors that give rise to scapegoat claims and the main safeguards to protect your position.

1. A client concession

A major concession made by your client is prime scapegoat territory.

Whenever your client gives something up—such as a legal right, bargaining chip or strategic option—they may regret it later and try to blame you for the consequences; typically, a large financial loss.

Stripping away the posturing and legal jargon, the dispute typically goes like this:

Client: You should have warned me I would lose out if I gave up X, Y and Z, in which case I would never have done that.

Advisor: You were given full advice about the risks, but you proceeded nonetheless.

Client: I disagree. Why would I ever *knowingly* have given up X, Y and Z? That would never have been in my best interests.

Advisor: We advised you about the risks during the negotiation meeting on *ABC* date, but you took a commercial decision to proceed despite our concerns.

Client: I deny you ever warned me about this. *Show me the evidence.*

We now reach a parting of the ways for the advisor:

Advisor: (1) Please see the email from our Mr D to you on *ABC* date that recorded our advice about the risks involved in giving up X, Y and Z.

OR

(2) Our Mr D has a firm recollection of having

advised you about this point at the meeting on *ABC* date, and of you deciding to proceed regardless.

In Scenario 1, the advisor can refute the claim before it has really begun. Case closed.

However, in Scenario 2 there will be contested witness evidence about what was or was not said at the meeting. If the claim reaches trial, the client may receive the benefit of any doubt because the onus is on the professional to record their advice. At best, an expensive settlement looms.

The following two examples show how opposite ways of handling a client concession can lead to drastically different outcomes.

In the first case, a wholesale toy supplier needed product liability insurance against the risk of their toys being defective and dangerous. The supplier's insurance broker found a suitable product liability policy, and also recommended product recall insurance to cover the supplier's losses if their products were ever withdrawn from sale due to health and safety concerns. The supplier, confident in their products, declined to take this additional product recall coverage.

Some months later, a product safety scare made national headlines. The supplier's top-selling toys were withdrawn from sale, immediately and indefinitely. The supplier's losses ran to many millions. Although the supplier tried to claim on their insurance, their insurers invoked the policy exclusion for product recall losses.

The supplier's last resort was a claim against their broker, saying, 'You negligently failed to ensure we were covered against product recall losses.' Was the claim bound to fail? Yes, the claim was dead in the water after one round of correspondence, but only because the broker had recorded their advice and the supplier's fateful decision, which was a client concession.

In the second case, a leading law firm succumbed to a scapegoat claim at a cost of several million pounds. The lawyer's client had planned to sue one of their trading partners for breach of contract. The client had two potential claims; one was simple, the other complex.

When the lawyer was first consulted, the simple claim was three months away from becoming time-barred due to the expiry of a statutory limitation period. They explained that this meant the client risked losing the right to bring the simple claim unless they sued before that deadline or secured a 'standstill' agreement to preserve their right to sue. However, the client said that for 'commercial reasons' they did not intend to pursue the simple claim, nor would they request any standstill agreement. They simply said that they would evaluate the complex claim in due course. This was a form of client concession.

The client returned to the lawyer five months later, determined to bring litigation against their trading partner. Lo and behold, they wanted to bring the simple claim. When the lawyer reiterated their earlier advice and explained the simple claim was now time-barred, the client sued the lawyer, alleging a negligent failure to protect the client's position.

The lawyer was adamant they had warned the client about the limitation date. However, they had no file note to prove it and their emails to the client merely chased for a decision about how the client wished to proceed. The lawyer's time recording narratives were equally inconclusive, so it became their word against their client's. After an indignant tussle, the case resulted in a multimillion-pound settlement.

* * *

Of course, there is nothing inherently problematic about clients making concessions; it happens all the time. This is the client's prerogative and they may have perfectly good reasons for doing so. However, these examples show how you could fall into a claim situation even though you gave the right advice.

Are there particular kinds of client concession that are more likely to give rise to a claim?

Although this varies according to your profession and specialism, there is one rule of thumb: the more significant and inexplicable your client's concession, the more likely it is to rebound on you later.

Where the court can see that a concession made some logical and commercial sense, even if it turned out badly, your client may struggle to prove any failure on your part. However, if you cannot plausibly explain why the client made the concession, you may face greater difficulty.

Unless you have clear evidence of your advice (or you can establish you had no duty to advise on the concession, perhaps because it was a purely commercial matter) it will be harder to defend the claim.

A habit of asking yourself 'Is my client giving anything up?' and answering from a broad perspective, will prompt you to make especially detailed notes when your client makes a major concession. When it comes to defending scapegoat claims, written records are crucial.

2. The Opportunist

Even the most challenging client does not *set out* to cause trouble for you. However, a client who acts opportunistically will be the most likely to sue your firm if they ever see a reason or opportunity to do so.

As explained in Chapter 5, the Opportunist may face a genuine problem that they then exploit to engineer and exaggerate a claim if they see a chance to extract money from your firm and its insurers.

Begin by asking yourself this question:

> Which of my clients, if they were to suffer a large loss, would be most likely to try to blame me and sue my firm, even though the loss was not my fault?

In answering that question, the surest sign of your clients' future behaviour is how they behave right now, so exercise caution with clients who:

- act unreasonably, disingenuously or dishonestly towards others;

- have already sacked a string of other advisors;

- put pressure on you to change your advice; or

- make it hard for you to do your job properly.

Effective communication is key at all levels. If you are in a supervisory role, make sure that your team knows the importance of keeping you properly informed, as this could prevent the situation from getting out of control. If you report to someone, take the initiative by informing them about such matters.

Sometimes you can identify this warning sign in a prospective client. If so, consider carefully whether the fee revenue will justify the risks involved in acting for them.

If you do find yourself advising an Opportunist, take particular care to:

- give ultra-clear advice;

- check that you have a signed engagement letter that defines the exact scope of your retainer;

- ensure that your reporting lines are clearly defined;

- copy your advice to your ultimate client, even if you are taking instructions from their agent; and

- keep detailed file notes as they are your best protection if you ever face a claim.

3. Fuzzy engagement

Regrettably, lawsuits against professional firms often reveal that they have no engagement letter, let alone one that records in detail the scope of their retainer. Naturally, this jeopardizes the firm's defence prospects.

As a preliminary matter, the engagement letter will define who exactly is your client; something that might seem simple, but which can be unclear and contentious in some cases.

The engagement letter will also contain a raft of provisions designed to protect your firm. Although there are some exceptions, this will typically include a contractual limitation of liability, which (subject to any questions of enforceability in some instances) could be crucial in reducing your firm's potential exposure.

An engagement letter is also crucial for another reason: by defining the scope of your engagement, it establishes limits upon the work that you are required to perform.

The fundamental question of the scope of the advisor's duty becomes a key battleground in many claims, as the court needs to determine:

- the advisor's precise scope of duty;

- whether that duty has been breached, and

- if so, whether the client has suffered losses that the advisor should have protected them against.

This means that if you were ever to face a claim, your firm's defence could be undermined by any ambiguity in the scope of the engagement, even if you are confident that you fulfilled your duty.

This difficulty arose for a law firm that advised two founders of the Eden Project, an environmental visitor attraction in Cornwall, England. As a visionary development that coincided with the turn of the new millennium, the project secured public funding from the UK National Lottery Fund. The lawyers advised the founders about preliminary matters, before establishing a charitable trust structure. The trust was required by the National Lottery funding rules in order to vest control in the hands of independent trustees who were duty-bound to run the project as a charity, rather than for private interests.

Although the project was successful, a dispute arose when the trustees refused to give the founders any share of the 'profits'. Although the founders protested, the trustees were acting correctly. In effect, the establishment of the trust structure meant the founders had lost any rights to profit from the project.

Faced with this problem, the founders sued their lawyers, alleging breach of a duty to protect their personal financial interests. The founders had made plain, they said, their expectation to profit from the venture, so their lawyers should have protected their rights before establishing any trust.

The lawyers defended the claim all the way to trial, adamant that they had never been retained to protect the founders' personal interests. Their instructions were limited, they said, to forming the trust structure and obtaining an option over land. They had advised the founders as promoters of the project rather than in their personal capacities.

However, the lawyers' defence was undermined by the lack of any engagement letter or other record of the scope of their retainer. The court accepted the founders' witness evidence that they had spoken of their expectations of making profits, and the court implied a duty upon the law firm to protect the founders' interests. Consequently, the firm was liable for damages of £1.8 million.

Crucially, the outcome would likely have been different if the firm had produced documentary evidence of a more limited engagement.

4. Inadequate notes

Every professional advisor knows the obvious importance of file notes, and yet a lack of notes is a recurring theme in professional liability lawsuits.

In Chapter 2, Robin faced exactly this problem as he could not prove the advice he had given to Derek. This undermined his firm's defence and led to a costly settlement. Such an experience is regrettably common.

In my training seminars, I am asked whether the format of the notes matters. In my view, it does not matter whether notes are typed or handwritten, so long as they are clear and comprehensive. However, where notes are handwritten, consider scanning them into your firm's document management system, especially where your advice has been significant or the client has made a concession.

Naturally, your written communications with the client, typically by email, should also contain notes of key points such as any major client concessions and the advice given in that respect.

Sometimes even WhatsApp messages have been crucial in defending liability claims, including an allegation of recklessness such as that levelled against Mr Moore in the introduction to this book. Like Mr Moore, the advisor was accused of not caring care about the accuracy of a report they were about to approve, and being willing to sign off on *anything* due to the volume of work on a deadline day. However, this allegation was refuted at trial by WhatsApp messages between the advisor and his colleague sent before dawn on the day in question. The messages, in which they debated issues relating to the draft report, showed a high level of diligence that was entirely inconsistent with the advisor having acted recklessly.

However, sensitive work communications should not ordinarily be made via WhatsApp or similar media, including for reasons of confidentiality.

Finally, in the event of a claim, your defence lawyer would also review your time records to see what work was done, when and by whom. Protect yourself further by noting key points of advice in your time-recording entries. If you sense a warning sign, such as a client concession that you have advised against, put this in your narratives. For example, if you have recorded, 'Telcon—advised about conceding X, Y and Z but client instructed us to proceed', this could provide a strong defence to any claim.

CHAPTER 8

'RED FLAGS' WITHIN YOUR WORK

E ven though scapegoat claims are prevalent, liability lawsuits arise more commonly from genuine errors and omissions. Therefore, protecting your practice also involves avoiding those errors that can lead to liability.

Experience suggests there are certain warning signs, or 'red flags', that can signal an elevated level of professional risk. This chapter addresses seven of those red flags which are recurring themes in lawsuits against advisory firms.

1. Crucial amendment

Mistaken amendments to a key term in a key document often lead to liability claims. But which documents and which terms are most significant?

Key documents are those that determine your client's rights and obligations or guide their future commercial decisions. This will often be a contract for the sale and purchase of an asset, such as a business, property or option. In other cases, the document is a report, statement or opinion that your client will rely upon when deciding whether to buy, sell, invest or take other action.

Such documents include valuation reports, audit opinions and references about a borrower's financial standing.

The key terms are those specific parts of a key document that actually determine the client's rights and obligations or inform their decision-making. Many times, the key clause is price, such as for Mr Ding in Chapter 3 where it was the crucial amendment to the pricing formula that led to a $1 billion claim.

> Making a crucial amendment could have a major impact on your client's position. Questions about your advice concerning the amendment, and your client's instructions, are ripe for dispute later.

2. Rotten Tooth

If your dentist treats one of your teeth and notices that another tooth is rotten, should they tell you even though you never asked for a general examination? Of course.

If the dentist *misses* the rotten tooth, do they fail in their duty to you, even though you never asked for a check-up? If they ought reasonably to have noticed the problem, then generally the answer would be 'yes'. Even though your dentist may have no duty to inspect your other teeth, if they look at them and notice—or should have noticed—something untoward, they will generally be under a duty to warn you. Broadly speaking, the same is true for professional advisors.

This very analogy has been endorsed by the English courts in a line of cases involving claims against lawyers. It would be prudent to assume that the principle also applies to other professions and in other jurisdictions, although there may be some exceptions.

As Laddie J held in *Credit Lyonnais SA v. Russell Jones and Walker* [2002] EWHC 310 (Ch):

> A solicitor is not a general insurer against his client's legal problems. His duties are defined by the terms of the agreed retainer ... although obligations may occasionally arise outside the terms of the retainer or where there is no retainer at all. Ignoring such exceptions, the solicitor only has to expend time and effort in what he has been engaged to do and for which the client has agreed to pay. He is under no general obligation to expend time and effort on an issue outside the retainer. However, if, in the course of doing that for which he is retained, he becomes aware of a risk or a potential risk to the client, it is his duty to inform the client. In doing that he is neither going beyond the scope of his instructions nor is he doing 'extra' work for which he is not to be paid. He is simply reporting back to the client on issues of concern which he learns of as a result of, and in the course of, carrying out his express instructions [...]
>
> [...] If a dentist is asked to treat a patient's tooth and, on looking into the latter's mouth, he notices that an adjacent tooth needs treatment, it is his duty to warn the patient

accordingly. So too, if in the course of carrying out instructions within his area of competence a lawyer notices or ought to notice a problem or risk for the client of which it is reasonable to assume the client may not be aware, the lawyer must warn him.

If you are ever uncertain about whether your client is already aware of a related issue that you have identified, protect yourself by raising the matter in writing.

3. Dabbling

You may be required to take on work that is beyond your expertise or address a highly unusual element of an otherwise typical engagement. Either way, this gives your insurers palpitations because dabbling increases your chances of making an error.

To address this dilemma, whenever you are about to advise on an important and unusual matter that is beyond your field of expertise, ask:

- Is there an expert within your firm?

- Can you refer it to a genuine specialist?

- If not, what additional precautions can you take to ensure that your advice is correct?

4. You do not understand

Although perhaps rare, some liability claims arise where the advisor simply did not understand the matter upon which they were advising.

In one such case, a law firm advised on a complex settlement of litigation between their client and a tax authority. Their client instructed their lawyers to settle all of the authority's claims so none of the tax demands would remain pending. However, the lawyers settled only part of the claims and left their client with an outstanding liability running into several million pounds. The resulting negligence claim went to trial and the judge held that the lawyers had not understood exactly what was being settled. The law firm was liable for damages of £7.65 million.

5. Late-night working

Long days and late nights are the bane of professional life. However, one suggestion is that if you amend a document late at night, check it again in the morning. Doing so could catch a mistake before it turns into a problem.

6. Especially technical work

In some claim situations, the advisory work was so technical that it was unsurprising that it led to an error.

Of course, many professional advisors thrive upon complexity and their clients require advice on difficult and technical matters. However, even though much of your work may be complex, some aspects are even more technical than others, in which case they represent elevated risk. When you are engaged in especially technical work, try to use a peer-review process where feasible.

One irony is that some highly technical work does not generate a level of fee income that would justify taking on the risks involved. In that case, if the workstreams are not central to your practice or your clients' needs, is it worthwhile to take on the engagement?

7. Dubious assumption

We each make assumptions every day and, although many are harmless, some assumptions could seriously harm your client's interests.

Naturally, the starting point is to establish that the client has given you all the necessary information in order for you to advise them and fulfil their instructions.

Beyond that basic point, claims can arise from unstated assumptions about:

- whether the client understands and appreciates your advice about a 'hidden pitfall' in a document that creates rights or obligations for the client;

- the meaning of a particular term in a document; or

- how a third party will act in the future.

Plainly, the first two assumptions can give rise to a claim if they turn out to be mistaken.

However, it is worth dwelling on the third assumption, about how a third party will act in the future. For example, you might be susceptible to making this assumption if it arises from how the third party has acted in the past. We will now see how a firm fell into this trap at a cost of several million dollars.

Whiston & Co were aviation brokers for Grantham LP, an offshore fund that wanted to buy a private jet for $23 million from the seller, an oligarch called Mr Chernaiev. The sale could not take place immediately as Grantham needed to secure funding for the purchase. So, the parties signed a conditional purchase contract that gave Grantham three months to complete the transfer. Mr Chernaiev had an option to withdraw if the deal was not completed by the longstop date.

However, the financial crisis intervened shortly after the parties signed the contract. Four months passed and, distracted by the crisis, neither Whistons nor Grantham nor Mr Chernaiev initially noticed the longstop date had passed. Once they realized that it had passed, Grantham still wanted to buy the jet and Mr Chernaiev still wanted to sell, so they agreed a two-month retrospective extension. Likewise, when the fresh deadline approached, the parties agreed a further extension of two months. So far, so good.

When the longstop date once again became imminent, Whistons tried to contact Mr Chernaiev for his agreement to a further extension. However, he did not respond and the deadline passed with no further extension having been agreed. At that stage, Whistons did not believe there was any problem and they did not raise the issue with Grantham. Whistons *assumed* that since Mr Chernaiev had agreed to two previous extensions, one more would be a mere formality.

However, this was a dangerous assumption as aircraft prices had risen in the meantime. Once the longstop date had passed, Mr Chernaiev wrote to Whistons, withdrawing from the contract. Although Mr Chernaiev *was* still willing to sell, he held Grantham over a barrel by demanding a $3 million uplift in the purchase price: take it or leave it.

Grantham had to choose between agreeing to the uplift or throwing away a similar sum in wasted funding and legal costs incurred to date. After taking legal advice, Grantham agreed to the uplift and brought a claim against Whistons for damages of $3 million plus costs. Grantham's case was that if Whistons had warned them of the impending deadline then Grantham would have completed the contract and avoided the $3 million uplift. Whistons had no good defence.

The Grantham case is a prime example of how a dubious assumption may result in a liability claim. What began as a commercial problem for the client, Grantham, became a lawsuit against their broker, Whistons. This happened because Whistons made the dubious assumption that a third party would behave in the same way as they had in the past. Rather than making this assumption, Whistons should have advised Grantham of the risk of Mr Chernaiev walking away unless they completed the contract by the longstop date, thereby putting that risk back on their client and protecting their own position.

CHAPTER 9

'RED FLAGS' WITHIN YOUR FIRM

W hereas the previous chapter concerned warning signs that may arise within your work, there are also indicators of elevated risk within your firm more generally.

This chapter addresses five such 'red flags' that could arise within your firm.

1. Divisions of responsibility

An internal division of responsibility, or a handover from one advisor to another, is a common cause of errors and oversights.

We saw a clear example of this difficulty in Chapter 1, where advisors from two departments of the same firm were working on contracts for Mr Berzin and the result was a mismatch between key terms.

This risk is heightened where multiple international offices of the firm are advising on the same matter in different time zones and with various reporting channels.

To reiterate, is everyone clear about the degree of overlap between individuals and departments, and who has final responsibility for key documents and advice?

2. Flaky Rainmaker

A Flaky Rainmaker is great at bringing in business for their firm, but less accomplished at performing the advisory work itself.

The Flaky Rainmaker usually takes one of two forms:

- the charismatic charmer whose technical skills leave something to be desired; or

- the busy leader who becomes a victim of their own success. Having risen to the top, they find themselves accepting too many engagements, and their supervision of more junior staff becomes too high-level.

In each case, mistakes can arise.

What protective measures can you take if you work with, or for, a Flaky Rainmaker?

If you are in a management role, consider introducing a peer-review process for everyone in your department, so that substandard work can be identified. That process could involve another partner reviewing specified documents—such as important contracts, reports or settlements—before they are completed.

If you are in a more junior role, take detailed notes of internal and client meetings and ensure that the scope of your own tasks and duties is clear.

3. Lone Ranger

While some Lone Rangers are simply quiet and competent professionals, others can cause problems.

One characteristic of a Lone Ranger is that they minimize discussions with their colleagues, which can lead to mistakes:

- A partner amends their associate's draft advice, reversing a key conclusion, and sends it to the client without discussing the amendment with the associate.

  ➢ Result: the partner's advice is wrong and the client suffers a large loss.

- A partner dominates their department so much that associates are wary of raising queries or concerns. A more junior member of the team is concerned that the partner's analysis is wrong. They cautiously raise a concern but are quickly dismissed and made to feel inadequate.

  ➢ Result: an avoidable mistake and an unhappy client.

- A partner insists on more junior team members preparing vacation handover notes, but does not do so themselves.

  ➤ Result: a deadline goes unnoticed and the client's position is prejudiced.

Some Lone Rangers are so protective of their client relationships that they prevent all interference and oversight. They may mask any problems and prevent anyone finding out about delays, missed deadlines or dubious advice—until a claim arises and the fallout begins.

Moreover, a small number of professional advisors are dishonest. They may abuse their position to defraud their clients, third parties or even their own firm. One example involves mortgage fraud, where lawyers and property surveyors collude with fraudsters to secure large loans via purchases of overvalued, or even non-existent, property.

If you are in a management position, notice if any colleague appears never to take a holiday, hand over a case or be the subject of proper oversight. Ensure that your firm is implementing regular internal file and accounting reviews.

4. Conflict Fudge

Every profession has its own rules about conflicts of interest; they form a part of standard risk management training and are not addressed here. However, one practical aspect may be overlooked: where a conflict of interest is 'fudged' rather than properly addressed.

This typically arises in response to a perceived commercial conflict, where one of your clients puts pressure on you to decline certain other work even though, strictly speaking, there is no conflict of interest. For example, a client may threaten to remove your firm from their panel of advisors or there is simply an unwritten rule that you must never act against them.

However, you want to take on new instructions wherever possible, so naturally you try to find a way around these commercial conflicts. Sometimes you will reach a solution that keeps everyone happy. But the result might be a Conflict Fudge that could backfire on your firm.

For example, imagine you are an attorney asked to represent a claimant, Tammy, in litigation against her bank and a fraudster called Roger. Tammy's bank had wrongfully transferred her money to Roger, so both the bank and Roger are potentially liable to Tammy.

However, as Tammy's bank is a client of your firm, there is a commercial conflict. You propose a solution: you will act for Tammy in her action against Roger, which she will bring first. If she recovers her loss from Roger, Tammy will not need to sue her bank. But if there is a shortfall, Tammy would then have to find another law firm to act in any claim against her bank. At face value, this arrangement makes sense.

However, as you progress the litigation against Roger, it becomes clear that Tammy will indeed need to sue the bank for breach of mandate. Another law firm brings that claim on her behalf, as planned, but the bank's defence rests upon a technical legal argument: that Tammy's prior legal action against Roger means she has ratified any breach of mandate by the bank. Tammy's other lawyers advise her to bring your firm into the action as co-defendant on the grounds that, if the bank's defence succeeds, it will have been your fault.

Even if you establish that the bank's defence is baseless, this might only be after protracted and costly litigation. The reality is that you had not addressed the risk of Tammy's claim against Roger prejudicing her lawsuit against the bank. Did the fact that you would never act against the bank blind you from looking at this question? In other words, was your judgement affected by the Conflict Fudge?

Not only does a Conflict Fudge increase your risk of oversights, but the arrangement may later be cast in a bad light by your client, especially where they have suffered a loss. They will invite the court to conclude that you put your firm's own interests above those of your client.

5. A Suspect Standard Practice

Standard practice is usually best practice, but not always. A standard practice may have developed within your firm (or more widely) despite having drawbacks that pose a risk to your clients. If such a risk materializes and a client loses money, the standard practice could come under close scrutiny. If the practice proves to be indefensible, your firm could be liable to the client for the resulting losses.

What makes a standard practice suspect? The presence of unnecessary risks for your clients. If the practice makes little sense from a client perspective, this is a warning sign for your firm, even if your profession generally follows the same practice.

Such a problem arose in Hong Kong in the 1980s.[1] The Privy Council found negligence by a firm of property conveyancing lawyers even though they had followed the prevailing market practice.

It had been customary for the buyer's lawyer simply to transfer the purchase funds to the seller's lawyer in advance of completion. However, the Privy Council held that this practice created foreseeable risks for the buyer, including the risk of embezzlement of funds by the seller or their lawyer. The buyer's lawyer had negligently failed to safeguard their client against those risks.

---

[1] *Wong (Edward) Finance Ltd v Johnson, Stokes and Master* [1984] AC 296.

At the very least, the buyer's lawyer should have made sure that the seller and their lawyer could not steal the amount of the purchase monies that ought to have been used to discharge the seller's mortgage. The buyer's lawyer could have addressed that risk simply by paying that sum directly to the secured lender, rather than to the seller or their lawyer.

As it was, the standard practice had become entrenched despite being suspect, and ultimately it was indefensible.

Therefore, consider whether your firm follows any standard practices that pose risks for your clients. If so, can you suggest a different practice that reduces or eliminates the client risks? Any such new practice might even become a market-leading innovation by you and your firm.

THE ADVISOR'S DEFENCE

Reflecting on the claims featured in this book, none of them were caused by general incompetence on the part of the professional advisors, and nor did they arise from the absence of any risk management policy. Firms have their risk policies in place, but the claims still come.

Broadly speaking, the claims fell into two categories. First, cases where complexity, fine margins and pressure meant something 'fell through the cracks'. Secondly, cases where the advisors were convinced that they gave the right advice but struggled to prove it.

As to the first category, plainly not all human error may be eliminated. However, a careful review of these cases reveals the claim scenario was never a foregone conclusion. Rather, indicators of elevated professional risk were either not identified or not adequately addressed.

As to the second category, seen as scapegoat claims, simple safeguards such as engagement letters and file notes were often lacking.

In each case there had been genuine scope to avoid the claim.

* * *

The main theme of *The Advisor's Minefield* is that we can best handle professional risk by drawing on a liability feedback loop to learn from claims brought against other advisors.

By way of summary, I recap the key lessons from my practice as defence counsel in lawsuits brought against leading professional firms.

First, liability claims arise from clients' problems, which take many forms and may arise at any time, including long after professional advice was given. The most common problems giving rise to claims are where a client:

(1) acquires a defective asset;

(2) faces a demand from a third party; or

(3) loses a valuable right.

Naturally, the specific risks will vary according to your profession, specialism and client base.

Secondly, the roots of a scapegoat claim often lie in a client concession for which the client later blames their advisors. A clearly defined scope of engagement and detailed file notes are the core protections against scapegoat claims.

Thirdly, 'red flags' may arise within your practice that signal an elevated risk of making an error; in particular where your work involves:

(1) making a crucial amendment to a key document affecting a client's rights or obligations;

(2) a Rotten Tooth, involving a related issue upon which a client has not expressly sought your advice;

(3) dabbling outside your field of expertise;

(4) handling matters you do not fully understand;

(5) working late at night;

(6) performing especially technical work; or

(7) making a dubious assumption.

Likewise, 'red flags' may arise within your firm, such as:

(1) a handover or internal division of responsibility;

(2) a Flaky Rainmaker;

(3) a Lone Ranger;

(4) a Conflict Fudge; or

(5) a Suspect Standard Practice.

Finally, my advice is to routinely tick as many boxes as possible on any defence lawyer's wish-list, starting with the basics:

- evidence of who exactly your client is;

- a clear record of the scope of your engagement;

- evidence of agreed reporting channels;

- clear and comprehensive records of your advice and/or your actions that will prove you performed your duties correctly; and

- time narratives showing what work you performed and when, and ideally capturing the essence of key advice and client instructions.

I truly hope you never face a claim but, if you do, these are the things your defence lawyer will need from you.

* * *

In conclusion, professional advisory firms are sued far more frequently than practitioners may imagine, and the costs are immense. However, many lawsuits may be avoided, or robustly defended, if the right safeguards are taken at the right time.

By aligning your technical expertise with an astute approach towards professional risk, you will be well equipped to protect your practice throughout your professional career.

NEXT STEPS

As your first follow-up action, I recommend completing the *Practice Defence Checklist*, which is available to all readers of *The Advisor's Minefield*.

The *Practice Defence Checklist* contains a short series of questions that help you identify the higher-risk aspects of your own practice right now.

To obtain your copy, please visit www.practice-checklist.com or use this QR code:

I also invite you to visit www.advisorsminefield.com for related content including expert interviews and emerging trends on the *Advisor's Minefield* podcast:

FIRM-WIDE IMPLEMENTATION

To best safeguard your firm, each member of the firm's advisory staff should know why major lawsuits arise in their field of practice and act in ways that protect the firm on a daily basis.

One foundational step is to ensure that each practitioner is familiar with *The Advisor's Minefield*, so I encourage you to roll out this book across your firm's professional advisory teams on a licensed basis, whether in hard copy, e-book or audiobook format.

You may also strengthen your firm's existing measures by making use of the Elite Professional Risk training courses that address these concerns in a targeted and engaging way for maximum impact.

This training delves deeper into the practice-specific factors that lead to lawsuits, resulting in improved awareness and decision-making at all levels of the firm.

For enquiries and bookings please visit: www.eliteprofessionalrisk.com

SHAUN TRACEY

Shaun Tracey, MCIArb, is a lawyer, speaker and author who defends professional advisory firms against high-value lawsuits and helps firms to avoid litigation.

As a lawyer, Shaun practices commercial litigation and arbitration at Campbells LLP. His practice includes defending leading professional firms against 'big-money' lawsuits, including claims against law firms, accountants, financial services firms, brokers and company directors. Notably, Shaun has been a key member of the legal team that successfully defended a major bank against a US$2 billion claim arising from the Madoff fraud. He also serves as Secretary of the Caribbean Branch of the Chartered Institute of Arbitrators.

Earlier in his career, Shaun practised in the market-leading Insurance & Professional Risk team at Simmons & Simmons LLP in London. He was also seconded to the professional indemnity claims department of Travelers insurance company where he handled a wide range of liability claims.

Shaun also practised as a commercial lawyer at Simmons & Simmons, advising on projects that included a £13 billion contract for air-to-air refuelling aircraft. This means that he understands the pressures and complexities of advising on major deals, as well as the fallout from liability claims.

As a speaker, Shaun delivers keynote speeches, seminars and expert training courses for professional firms to help them avoid high-cost litigation.

Shaun also serves as President of the Cayman Islands Chess Federation and is the founder of a national Chess in Education programme. Shaun is a Candidate Master and has represented his country twice at the FIDE Chess Olympiad.